This Book Belongs to:

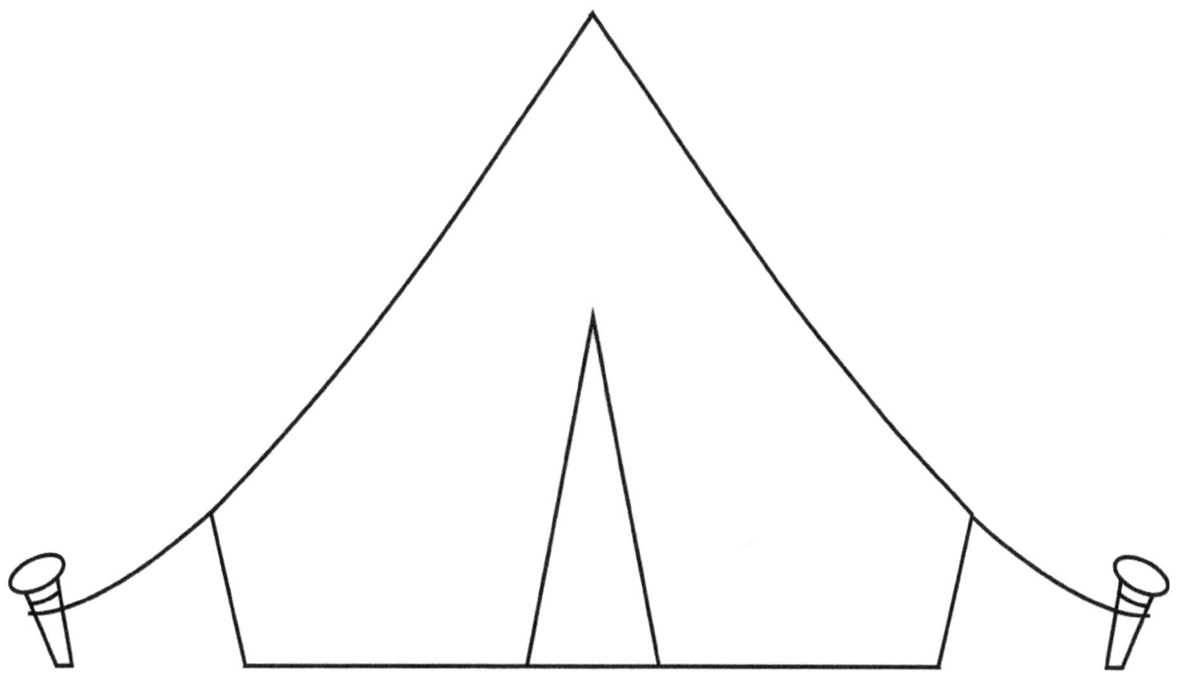

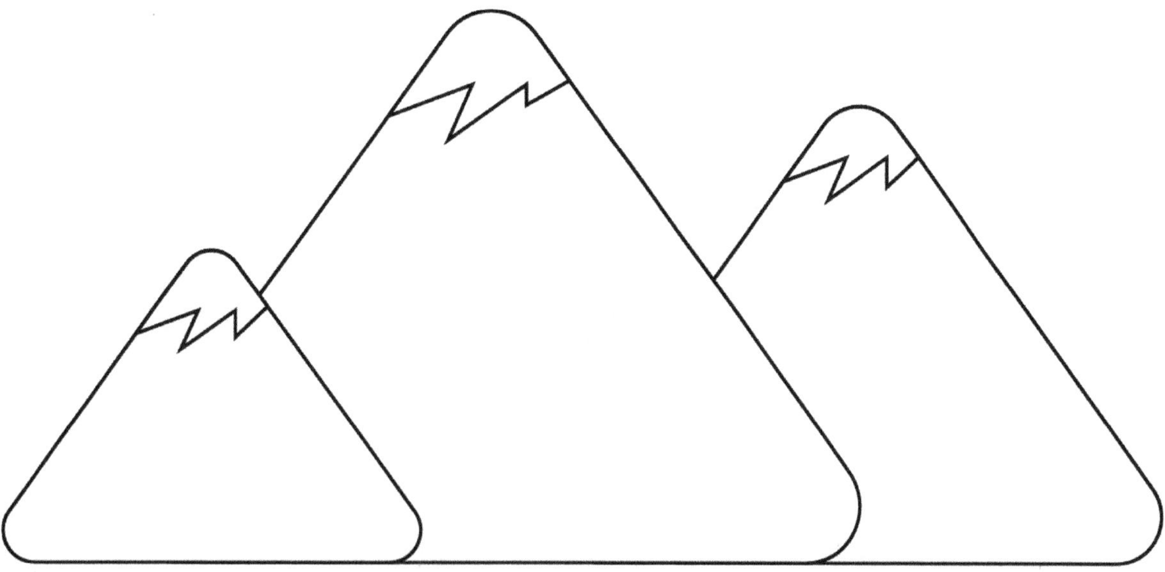

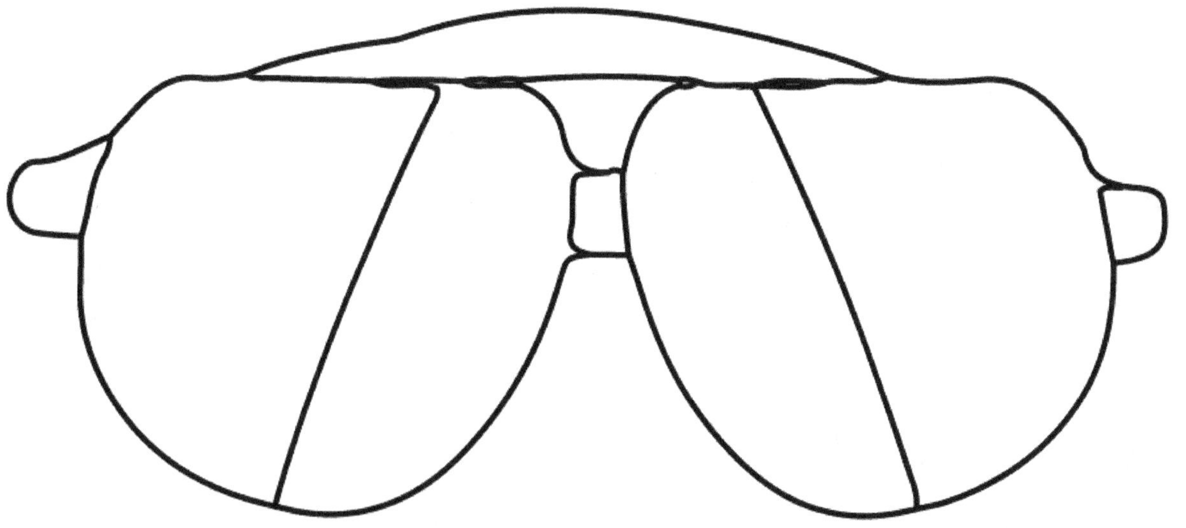

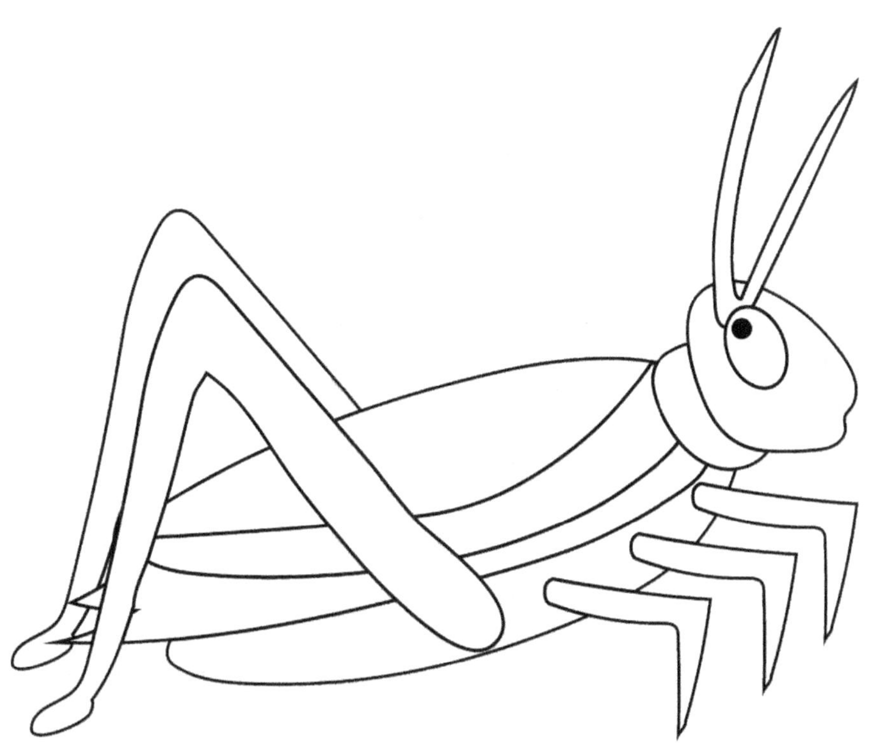

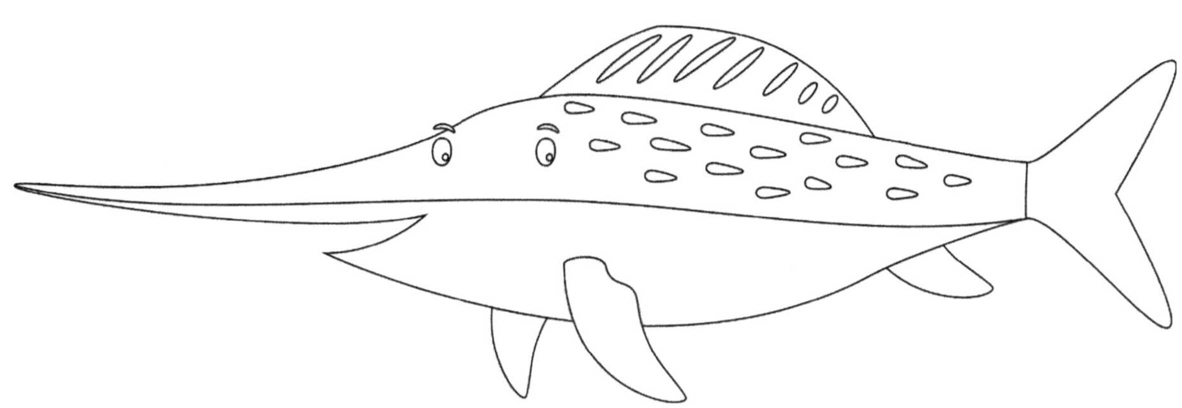

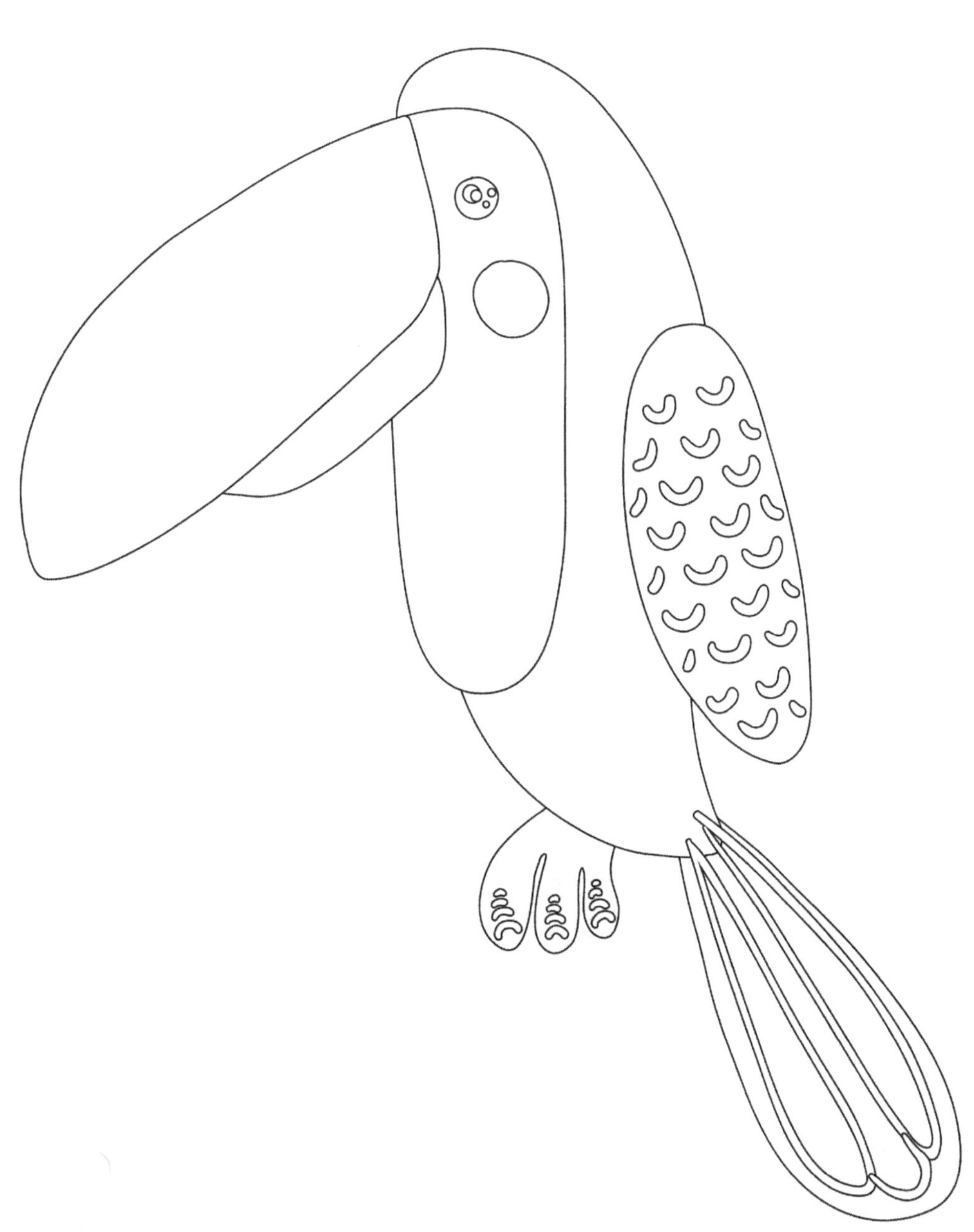

www.ingramcontent.com/pod-product-compliance
Lightning Source LLC
Chambersburg PA
CBHW081624250726
48657CB00009B/2717